SPIDERS

TRAPDOOR SPIDERS

James E. Gerholdt
ABDO & Daughters

Published by Abdo & Daughters, 4940 Viking Drive, Suite 622, Edina, Minnesota 55435.

Library bound edition distributed by Rockbottom Books, Pentagon Tower, P.O. Box 36036, Minneapolis, Minnesota 55435.

Printed in the United States.

Cover Photo credit: Peter Arnold, Inc.
Interior Photo credits: Peter Arnold, Inc. pages 13, 15, 17, 19
James Gerholdt pages 5, 7, 9, 11,21
Pages 7 & 11 courtesy of Black Hills Reptile Gardens.

Pages 7, 11, 21 courtesy of Spineless Wonders.

Edited by Julie Berg

Library of Congress Cataloging-in-Publication Data

Gerholdt, James E., 1943
Trapdoor Spiders / by James E. Gerholdt.
    p. cm. — (Spiders)
Includes bibliographical references (p.24) and Index.
   ISBN 1-56239-509-2
1. Trapdoor spiders—Juvenile literature. [1. Trapdoor spiders. 2. Spiders.] I. Title. II.
Series: Gerholdt, James E., 1943- Spiders.
QL458.4.G46   1995
595.4'4—dc20   95-14021
                                                       CIP
                                                       AC

About the Author

Jim Gerholdt has been studying reptiles and amphibians for more than 40 years. He has presented lectures and displays throughout the state of Minnesota for 9 years. He is a founding member of the Minnesota Herpetological Society and is active in conservation issues involving reptiles and amphibians in India and Aruba, as well as Minnesota.

Contents

TRAPDOOR SPIDERS

A spider is an **arachnid**. It has two body parts and eight legs. All arachnids are **arthropods**. Their skeletons are on the outside of their bodies. Trapdoor spiders are also **ectothermic**. They get their body temperature from the **environment**.

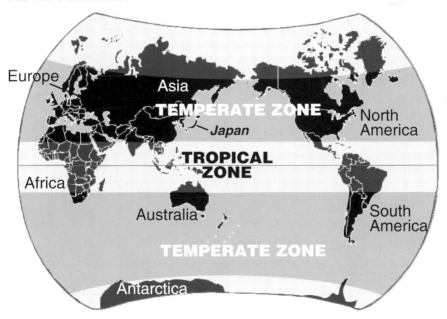

Trapdoor spiders are found in the Earth's temperate (warm) and tropical (hot) zones.

This red African trapdoor spider will make a burrow with a tight-fitting "door."

Trapdoor spiders are found in Southeast Asia, Japan, and most warm parts of the world. They are called trapdoor spiders because of the **burrows** they make, which usually has a "door" that closes tightly.

SIZES

Trapdoor spiders are fairly large. Many **species** reach a body length of over one inch (2.5 cm). The California trapdoor spider is larger. A smaller species, like the ravine trapdoor spider, may only reach a length of one inch (2.5 cm).

The red African trapdoor spider is another large species. It can reach a length of over 1.5 inches (4 cm). The legspan, the distance measured across the legs, is about twice the length of the body.

The legspan of the trapdoor spider is twice the length of its body.

SHAPES

Trapdoor spiders are very heavy bodied. They are also hairy. They have two body parts that are almost round in shape. The front is called the **cephalothorax.** It is made up of the head and **thorax**. The rear body part is called the **abdomen**, where the **spinnerets** are found. The spinnerets make the spider's silk.

There are eight legs attached to the front of the body, along with the **pedipalps**, which look like two short legs.

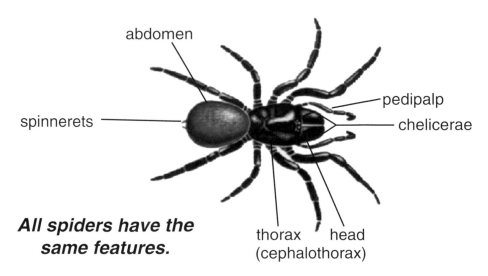

abdomen

pedipalp

spinnerets

chelicerae

All spiders have the same features.

thorax (cephalothorax)

head

8

The two body parts can be seen on this red African trapdoor spider.

These are used to grab the spider's **prey**. Between the **pedipalps** are the **chelicerae**, to which the fangs are attached. There are also **spines** on the chelicerae, which are used for digging the spider's **burrow**.

COLORS

All trapdoor spiders have similar colors. A typical **species**, like the California trapdoor spider has a brown or tannish **abdomen**, a dark brown **cephalothorax**, and darker legs and **chelicerae**.

The red African trapdoor spider has a reddish shade to its legs and chelicerae, with a reddish brown cephalothorax and tan abdomen. There is also a wide darker stripe on the abdomen.

A California trapdoor spider.

WHERE THEY LIVE

Trapdoor spiders spend most of their time in the ground. This is where they have made their **burrows**, with tight-fitting doors. Different **species** have different kinds of burrows and doors. One type of door is called a wafer door. It is made of silk spun by the spider.

The other type of door is called a cork door. It is made of silk and **debris**. These doors fit so well that they are hard for humans or enemies to see. Some burrows are dug straight down into the ground. Others have side rooms. Each species has its own design.

A cross-section photograph of a trapdoor spider in its burrow. The entrance (right) is plugged with silk and debris.

SENSES

Trapdoor spiders have the same five senses as humans. Like most spiders, they have eight eyes. But their eyesight is not very sharp. Since they spend most of their time in **burrows**, good eyesight is not important.

The most important sense a trapdoor spider has is its ability to feel **vibrations**. The hairs on its legs and **pedipalps** sense the vibrations. Trapdoors can also taste and smell the world around them with their mouth and the ends of their legs and pedipalps.

*The hairs on the legs of this trapdoor
spider sense vibrations.*

DEFENSE

The most important defense a trapdoor spider has against its enemies is its **burrow**. This is where the spider spends most of its time. If an enemy tries to get through the burrow's door, the spider holds it shut with its **chelicerae**.

The ravine trapdoor spider, from the southeastern United States, has a hardened **abdomen** that is rounded on the rear. It will retreat into its burrow, shut the door, and go to the bottom of the burrow. There, the hardened rear of the abdomen makes a perfect plug. This gives it two different defenses.

The most important defense a trapdoor spider has against enemies is its burrow. When threatened, the spider will close the door.

FOOD

Trapdoor spiders eat all types of insects, including beetles, ants, and grasshoppers. Small **vertebrates** like lizards are also eaten.

As the spider waits in its **burrow**, it can feel the **vibrations** from nearby **prey**. The spider will then leap out and grab the prey. It is then taken into the burrow where it is eaten. Females seldom leave the burrow. Males may wander out after a rain storm has passed.

As the trapdoor spider waits in its burrow, it can feel the vibrations from nearby prey. The spider will then leap out and grab the prey.

BABIES

All trapdoor spiders hatch from eggs that have been laid by the female. Once the eggs have been laid in an egg case, she will usually guard them. Without the proper heat and **humidity**, the eggs will not hatch.

After hatching, the baby spiders will sometimes stay near the female, but soon go their own way. As they grow, the babies shed their skin. This is called **moulting**. It is often hard to tell the skin from the spider who shed it!

The female trapdoor spider guards her eggs until they hatch.

GLOSSARY

Abdomen (AB-do-men) - The rear body part of an arachnid.

Arachnid (uh-RACK-nid) - An arthropod with two body parts and eight legs.

Arthropod (ARTH-row-pod) - An animal with its skeleton on the outside of its body.

Burrow - A hole or tunnel dug into the ground.

Cephalothorax (seff-al-o-THORE-ax) - The front body part of an arachnid.

Chelicerae (kel-ISS-err-eye) - The leg-like organs of a spider that have the fangs attached to them.

Debris (duh-BREE) - Scattered remains of something broken or destroyed.

Ectothermic (ek-toe-THERM-ik) - Regulating body temperature from an outside source.

Environment (en-VI-ron-ment) - Surroundings an animal lives in.

Habitat - An area an animal lives in.

Humidity - The amount of water in the air.

Moulting (MOLE-ting) - The act of shedding the old skin.

Pedipalps (PED-uh-palps) - The two long sense organs on the head of an arachnid.

Prey - Animals eaten by other animals.

Species (SPEE-seas) - A kind or type.

Spine - A pointy spike on the spider's chelicerae which is used to dig.

Spinnerets (spin-err-ETS) - The two body parts attached to the abdomen of a spider where the silk comes out of.

Thorax (THORE-axe) - A section of the front body part of an arachnid.

Vertebrate (VER-tuh-brit) - An animal with a backbone.

Vibration (vie-BRAY-shun) - Rapid movement up and down or back and forth.

Index

BIBLIOGRAPHY

Kaston, B. J. *How to Know the Spiders*. William C. Brown Co., 1953.

Levi, Herbert W. and Lorna R. *Spiders and Their Kin*. Golden Press, 1990.

Milne, Lorus and Margery. *The Audubon Society Field Guide to North American Insects and Spiders*. Alfred A. Knopf, 1980.

O'Toole, Christopher (editor). *The Encyclopedia of Insects*. Facts On File, Inc., 1986.

Preston-Mafham, Rod and Ken. *Spiders of the World*. Facts On File, Inc., 1984.